THOUGHTFULNESS THINKING

Mindfulness

VICKY BUREAU
M.S., SCHOOL COUNSELING

A Starfish Book

SEAHORSE
PUBLISHING

Teaching Tips for Caregivers:

As a caregiver, you can help your child succeed in school by giving them a strong foundation in language and literacy skills and a desire to learn to read.

This book helps children grow by letting them practice reading skills.

Reading for pleasure and interest will help your child to develop reading skills and will give your child the opportunity to practice these skills in meaningful ways.

- Encourage your child to read on her own at home
- Encourage your child to practice reading aloud
- Encourage activities that require reading
- Establish a reading time
- Talk with your child
- Give your child writing materials

Teaching Tips for Teachers:

Research shows that one of the best ways for students to learn a new topic is to read about it.

Before Reading

- Read the "Words to Know" and discuss the meaning of each word.
- Read the back cover to see what the book is about.

During Reading

- When a student gets to a word that is unknown, ask them to look at the rest of the sentence to find clues to help with the meaning of the unknown word.
- Ask the student to write down any pages of the book that were confusing to them.

After Reading

- Discuss the main idea of the book.
- Ask students to give one detail that they learned in the book by showing a text dependent answer from the book.

TABLE OF CONTENTS

Mindfulness: Do You Have It?

What happens when you wake up in the morning?

Is it **rush**, rush, rush?

Or go, go, go?

What if you slowed things down?

Would you have time to smell the pancakes?

Or **notice** the coolness of your toothpaste?

Today’s world goes by so fast!

Can you remember what you ate for lunch yesterday?

Or what you learned in
art class last Tuesday?

Do you ever feel like there is just too much to get done and not enough time to do it?

When was the last time you stopped, slowed down, and became **mindful**?

What's the temperature in your room?

Are you cold under the covers?

Do you sing along to the music in the car?

Do you **savor** the chocolate chips in your cookie?

Mindfulness: What Does It Mean?

If you close your eyes, what do you see? Yes, it might look dark.

But in order to truly see what's around you, you have to feel what's around you.

It may be hard to stay **focused**. But closing your eyes and **appreciating** what's around you is how you **grow** to be mindful!

It may not be easy...

...but it's always worth it.

Because YOU are worth it!

Try some of this, or **explore** some of that.

Say more of this, or do less of that.

Look within YOU!

Mindfulness: How Can You Build Yours?

You can learn more about yourself! Want to know how? Close your eyes.

Smell what's around you.

Feel what's around you.

Hear what's around you.

Mindfulness takes time. And what's the rush?

WHAT WOULD YOU DO?

You're running late for school. When can you find a moment to be mindful?

Your schoolwork seems too hard. When can you find a moment to be mindful?

You're worried about an after-school activity. When can you find a moment to be mindful?

Words to Know

appreciating (uh-PREE-shee-ate-ing): understanding the value of something

explore (ik-SPLOR): to search through or look into

focused (FOH-kuhsd): concentrated on your thoughts; not distracted

grow (gro): to spring up and develop to maturity

mindful (MINDE-ful): paying full attention to something

notice (NOH-tis): to see or become aware of something

rush (rush): to perform in a short time or at high speed

savor (SAY-vur): to notice, appreciate, and enjoy a taste, a smell, or another experience

Index

Comprehension Questions

1. How can you show mindfulness even when it's hard to focus?

2. What are some things you can do to help you build mindfulness?

3. How does a person's mindfulness affect their appreciation?

4. What is the difference between being focused and being mindful?

About the Author

Vicky Bureau was born in Longueuil, Quebec, and was raised in South Florida. As a teacher, she developed a passion for the social and emotional growth of her students and later transitioned into the area of child and adolescent psychology after earning her master's degree in school counseling. In addition to working with children, Vicky loves to be surrounded by animals and nature. She lives in Fort Lauderdale with her family: Billy, Khloe, M.J., and Max; her three cats, Alley, Baguette, and Salem; and her dog, Boomer.

Written by: Vicky Bureau
Design by: Under the Oaks Media
Editor: Kim Thompson

Library of Congress PCN Data
Mindfulness / Vicky Bureau
Thoughtfulness Thinking
ISBN 978-1-63897-092-7 (hard cover)
ISBN 978-1-63897-178-8 (paperback)
ISBN 978-1-63897-264-8 (EPUB)
ISBN 978-1-63897-350-8 (eBook)
Library of Congress Control Number: 2021945227

Printed in the United States of America.

Photographs/Shutterstock: Benjavisa Ruangvaree: cover, p. 1; luchioly: p. 4; Kwanchai.c; Maria Spb; p. 6; Africa Studio: p. 7, 19c; Pixel_Shot: p. 8; Pressmaster: p. 9; Diego Cerro: p. 10; Dziurek: p. 11a; martellostudio: p. 11b; Torychemistry: p. 13; gabczi: p. 14; monkeybusinessimages: p. 15, 17b; ESBProfessional: p. 16a; Rido: p. 16b; VP Photo Studio: p. 17a; Brocreative: p. 17c; Daria Grebenchuk:p. 19a; Serhii Bobyk: p. 19b: Serhii Bobyk

Seahorse Publishing Company
www.seahorsepub.com

Published in the United States
Seahorse Publishing
PO Box 771325
Coral Springs, FL 33077

SEAHORSE PUBLISHING